Rhode Island Fish Species

Game Fish & Panfish

Billy Grinslott & Kinsey Marie Books

ISBN - 9781968228682

Banded Sunfish got their name because they have darker lines that run vertically on their sides. They also have a rounded tail with spots on their body, tail and fins. Banded sunfish are typically only about 2 inches long, making them one of the smallest sunfish. Their small size makes them vulnerable to larger fish, so they thrive in protected areas. Banded sunfish prefer slow-moving, vegetated waters like swamps, ponds, and backwaters of creeks

The Green Sunfish is blue green in color. It has yellow flecks on both its scales and some parts of its sides. The Green Sunfish also has broken blue stripes which is why some people confuse it with the Bluegill. Green Sunfish are very adaptable. They can live in any body of water that has vegetation or weeds. Green sunfish are opportunistic feeders, consuming insects, small fish, and other invertebrates.

The bluegill also considered a sunfish is the most popular fish to fish for. They are called pan fish because they are about the size of a frying pan. Bluegills love to eat insects and bugs. They have good vision and rely on their keen eyesight to feed. Three types in this group are the Bluegill, Sunfish, and Pumpkinseed. The largest bluegill caught in Rhode Island was 2 pounds, 1 ounce.

The Warmouth is a member of the Rock Bass, Green Sunfish and Bluegill family. They can survive in low oxygen environments while other fish cannot. Warmouth can thrive in muddy water, when other fish can't. Warmouth are often confused with rock bass. The difference between the two is in the anal fin: warmouth have three spines on the anal fin ray and rock bass have six spines.

The Redbreast sunfish has a red-yellow chest and belly with rusty brown spots on their body. The species is known for its distinctive grunting vocalizations, which are produced by grinding their teeth together. Redbreast sunfish can survive in oxygen-poor environments by using their gills to extract oxygen from air bubbles trapped in aquatic vegetation.

The Pumpkinseed is also known as pond perch, sun perch, and punky's sunfish. It can be found in numerous lakes, ponds, and rivers. It is their body shape resembling the seed of a pumpkin, that inspired their name. Pumpkinseed sunfish have speckles on their orangish colored sides and back, with a yellow to orange belly and chest. They are active during the day and rest at night near the bottom or in shelter areas.

The Blue spotted sunfish is a small freshwater fish known for its vibrant blue spots and tolerance for acidic low oxygen waters. They are native to the southeastern and eastern United States, inhabiting ponds, rivers, and backwaters with dense vegetation. They are one of the smallest fish in their family, typically reaching a maximum length of about 3.7 inches. Both males and females have light blue or white spots, but males tend to have more intense and vibrant spotting. They have a relatively short lifespan, typically living around 5 years.

The Mud Sunfish is a secretive, small freshwater fish known for its stocky body, large mouth, and distinctive dark stripes. It prefers to live in slow-moving, tannin-stained waters like swamps, bogs, ponds, and backwaters with soft, silty bottoms and aquatic plants. Their color ranges from olive to brownish tan. They are usually small, rarely exceeding 6 to 8 inches in length.

The American shad is the largest species in the herring family. They are known for a delicate, rich flavor, often described as oily or like sardines. They can grow up to 30 inches and weigh up to 12 pounds. They have a metallic blue/green back, silver sides, a deeply forked tail, and a row of dark spots behind the gill flap. They prefer freshwater rivers for spawning and the Atlantic Ocean for feeding, often traveling hundreds of miles upstream. The largest American shad officially recorded in Rhode Island was 25 inches long.

The Atlantic tomcod is a small, bottom-dwelling fish species, also known as a frostfish. They have a slender body, three dorsal fins, two anal fins, a rounded tail. Some people call the Atlantic cod a tomcod, but they are different. While they are related members of the same cod family, they are different species with distinct sizes, habitats, and physical traits, with the tomcod being much smaller and preferring shallow, brackish coastal waters.

White perch grow seven to ten inches in length and rarely weigh more than one pound. They have a silvery body with faint lines on the sides. The white perch is an opportunistic feeder. Young feed primarily on zooplankton and adults feed on aquatic insect larvae, minnows and fish eggs. White Perch is a euryhaline species, inhabiting fresh, brackish and coastal waters. The record for the biggest white perch caught in Rhode Island is 2 pounds, 7.28 ounces.

The two most famous perches are the common perch and the yellow perch. The yellow perch has a brilliant greenish yellow color with orange fins. The yellow perch is the biggest one and can grow to a size of 18 inches. It's also known as the jumbo perch. The other type of perch is the white perch. The largest yellow perch caught in Rhode Island weighed 2 pounds, 4 ounces.

Alewives are anadromous fish that migrate from the ocean to freshwater rivers and streams to spawn. They are small, silvery herring-like fish with a saw-edged belly and a forked tail. Alewives have a distinctive saw-edge on their belly, formed by modified scales called scutes. This feature is used for protection and is also what gives them the nickname saw bellies. While most alewives are anadromous, there are also populations that have become landlocked.

Fallfish are the largest native minnow species in eastern North America, often reaching 15-18 inches in length and weighing over 2 pounds, inhabiting clear, rocky streams. They are known for building massive, pyramid-shaped nests from rocks, with males creating structures that can reach 6 feet in diameter and weigh up to 2 tons. They are silvery with dark-edged scales, a dark stripe along the back, and a large, blunt snout.

The Rock Bass is not actually a bass but a member of the sunfish family. They are commonly known as redeyes, due to their bright red to orangish iris, and are sometimes confused as smallmouth bass or warmouth. Rock bass prefer waters with rocky vegetated areas, that's how they got their name. Rock Bass rarely exceed 1–2 pounds.

There are two main types of crappies. The white crappie and the black crappie. They are also members of the sunfish family. The difference between the white and black crappie is one has dark spots and the other has dark lines and is lighter in color. The white crappie has six dorsal fin spines, whereas the black crappie has eight dorsal fin spines. The white crappie can grow bigger and more of the bigger white crappie are caught in North America. The record for the biggest crappie ever caught in Rhode Island is a 3-pound black crappie.

The sucker fish has the same mouth as a carp. They got their name because their mouth is like a suction cup. They normally are bottom feeders and suck their food from the bottom of the lake. Many people use sucker fish to fish for northern pike and other big game fish. The White Sucker is a common, large native sucker species, typically reaching 6 to 18 inches long.

The black, brown and yellow bullhead are part of the catfish family. They usually only grow to about 10 inches long. They use their whiskers to help find food. The bullhead is the most common member of the catfish family. Bullheads live in the water containing low oxygen levels. They can survive on low oxygen areas, where other fish can't. The Rhode Island state record for the largest bullhead (specifically a Brown Bullhead) is 4 pounds 9.44 ounces.

The Channel Catfish are the most fished catfish species with around 8 million anglers fishing for them per year. Channel catfish have taste buds all over their body, making them highly sensitive to the taste and smell of food. They also have barbels (whiskers) around their mouths, which are used for sensing and tasting food. They use sound waves to communicate with each other. They can also produce alarm substances to warn other catfish of danger. Channel catfish in Rhode Island typically range from 1 to 5 pounds and measure 12 to 20 inches.

The madtom is a small catfish that is native to the eastern United States. Madtoms are scaleless fishes with eight whisker-like barbels around their mouths used as sensors. The madtom feeds on the bottom at night, using its sensitive barbels, whiskers to touch and taste for food. Its diet consists mostly of aquatic insects.

White catfish are interesting because they are smaller than other common catfish species like channel catfish, they have a wider head and lack the black spots of channel catfish. White catfish are the smallest of the large North American catfish species. The White catfish has white chin barbells, which distinguish it from other species. There are four pairs of barbels, whiskers around the mouth, two on the chin, one at the angle of the mouth, and one behind the nostril. The biggest white catfish caught in Rhode Island weighed 16 pounds, 12 ounces.

The stonecat is a slender, freshwater catfish known for its preference for living in fast moving streams and rivers. They are often found under rocks and boulders in riffles. Stonecats have a long, thin body with a rounded or slightly forked tail. Their color varies, typically ranging from tan to gray on the back and sides, with a lighter belly. Stonecats are primarily active at night, feeding on insects, fish eggs, and small fish. Stonecats typically reach 4 to 8 inches in length and weigh up to 1 pound.

The American eel is North America's only freshwater eel, known for its snake-like body, and ability to live in freshwater. They have a Snake-like body, dark on top (green/brown) with yellowish sides and a pale belly. They have a continuous fin that runs along the length of their whole back. They use their whole body to swim and can slither like a snake over the ground and obstacles. They are most active at night and hide during the day, under rocks or burying themselves into the sediment at the bottom. American eels in Rhode Island commonly reach lengths of 2 to 3.5 feet.

Snakehead fish are known as walking fish, because they can move on land for days by wiggling with their fins and body. They can breathe air with lung-like organs, allowing them to survive out of water for days and even crawl to new water bodies using their fins. They can also burrow into the mud and hibernate during cold weather or dry spells. They thrive in various slow-moving, shallow, vegetated waters, like ponds, swamps, and streams, and can survive in low oxygen levels. Northern Snakehead fish in Rhode Island, typically grow to about 2 to 3 feet in length and can weigh 15-20 pounds.

The banded killifish is a small, slender, schooling fish found in clear, shallow, vegetated lakes, ponds, and slow-moving rivers. It is recognized by 10-20 vertical dark bars, a flat head, and an upward-turned mouth. They are schooling fish, often forming groups of 3–6 adults, while juveniles form larger groups of 8–12. They are primarily insectivores, eating aquatic insects, larvae, and small crustaceans.

Sculpins are small, bottom-dwelling fish with a flattened body shape, large pectoral fins, and a unique camouflage pattern, often found in clear, fast-flowing waters with rocky substrates, and they are known for their ambush hunting tactics. Sculpins have very large mouths and can swallow items nearly as large as themselves. Many sculpins have venomous spines along their fins, with particularly dangerous spines on their gill covers, used for defense.

Striped bass are often called Stripers. Striped bass live in both salt and fresh water. Striped bass have very sensitive eyes and will seek deep water when the sun is out. Striped bass have a preferred water temperature range of from 55° F to 68° F, and swim to find water of these temperatures. White Bass are related to Striped Bass and have lighter stripes on their sides. The biggest striped bass ever caught in Rhode Island is a 77-pound, 6.4-ounce fish.

Sturgeons have sharp spines on their back, so be careful when handling them. Instead of scales, sturgeon skin is covered in bony plates called scutes, which can be very sharp on young sturgeon. Sturgeons have been around since the dinosaur days. Sturgeons mostly live in large, freshwater lakes and rivers. Their average lifespan is 50 to 60 years. The Shortnose Sturgeon typically grows to 4.5 feet in length and can weigh up to 50 pounds.

Carp have long been an important food fish to humans. Carp are bottom feeders for the most part and their mouth is made like a suction cup, so they can suck food off the bottom. Carp are good for a lake because they help clean the bottom of the lake. A 40-pound, 40-inch carp caught in a Rhode Island pond in June 2020 is among the largest on record for the state.

The rainbow trout gets its name because of its brilliant colors. Rainbow trout populations are good indicators of water pollution because they can only survive in clean waters. They like to live in rivers and streams. Rainbow trout rank among the top five most sought game fish in North America. The biggest rainbow trout caught in Rhode Island is a 15-pound, 12-ounce fish.

The lake trout is one of the biggest of the trout family. The biggest lake trout caught was 72 pounds. Lake trout like to live in lakes that are deep. They like being in the cool water in the deep parts of a lake. They have been reported to live up to 70 years in some Canadian lakes. Lake trout are stocked in some areas of the state.

Brook trout are characterized by their olive-green bodies with pale, worm-like markings, red spots with bluish halos, and orange-red fins with white and black edges. They can grow up to 12 inches in length. Brook trout are cold-water fish that prefer clean, clear, and cold streams, lakes, and ponds. The largest Brook trout officially recorded in Rhode Island weighed 3 pounds 12 ounces and measured 21 inches in length.

Tiger trout are known for their aggressive nature and awesome looking tiger-like stripes. Tiger trout are not naturally occurring in the wild, but rather a hybrid created by mixing a female brown trout with a male brook trout. They are stocked in lakes and rivers. Their striking appearance with tiger-like stripes and patterns, makes them easily recognizable. They are known to grow faster than their parent species. Tiger trout in Rhode Island typically reach 10 to 16 inches in length.

Brown trout can live up to 20 years. Brown trout have a higher tolerance for warmer waters than either brook or rainbow trout. Brown trout can be found on almost every continent except Antarctica, and many can be found living in the ocean. They have olive-brown, yellow-orange, or silvery sides with a mix of black, red, and orange spots. The official state record for brown trout is often cited as a 19-pound, 12-ounce fish.

Atlantic salmon are anadromous, meaning they live in both freshwater and saltwater. Atlantic Salmon are present in Rhode Island, primarily as landlocked fish in inland lakes and tributaries rather than sea-run fish. They are known for their impressive leaping abilities, allowing them to jump over waterfalls and obstacles to reach spawning grounds. Atlantic salmon change color when they return to freshwater to spawn, becoming a rusty-bronze color with red markings. The biggest Atlantic salmon caught in Rhode Island weighed 22 pounds, 5.28 ounces.

The largemouth bass is the most sought-after bass in North America. Largemouth bass live in just about every lake in North America. They have great hearing and can hear a crayfish crawling on the bottom of the lake. The biggest largemouth bass ever caught in Rhode Island weighed 11 pounds, 3.2 ounces.

Smallmouth bass have a smaller mouth than the largemouth bass. They also have different markings and are lighter in color. They don't live in most lakes because they prefer living in colder water. They are typically found in the northern states in America because the water is cooler. The current world record smallmouth is an 11-pound, 15-ounce fish. They can be found in lakes, reservoirs, and rivers. The biggest Smallmouth bass ever caught in Rhode Island weighed 5 pounds, 15 ounces.

The walleye got its name because of its white looking eyes. Their eyes collect light, even in low light conditions. This means they can see in the dark. Because they can see in the dark, they mostly feed at night. During the daytime their eyes are very sensitive, so they usually head for deeper water or shady places. Walleye like to live in cooler water and are normally found in the upper part of North America. Walleye are stocked in certain lakes in Rhode Island.

Pickerel kind of look like northern pike, but they are not. The Pike is larger in size than the Pickerel. The Pickerel has more spots than the Pike, but the Pike has spots on its fins and pickerel don't. Pickerel has a dark bar beneath their eyes and northern pike don't. Pickerel are also known as gunfish or slime darts. The record for the largest Chain Pickerel caught in Rhode Island is 6 pounds, 14 ounces.

The Redfin Pickerel is a small, solitary freshwater fish in the pike family, typically measuring 10–15 inches and living 8–10 years. They inhabit clear, slow-moving, heavily vegetated streams and swamps. They are ambush predators feeding on small fish, crustaceans, and insects. They are olive to yellowish green with distinct, bright red-orange fins and a dark, backwards-slanting bar beneath the eye.

The Northern Pike is one of the most sought-after fish for anglers. It got its name because it likes to live in cooler water mainly in the northern states of North America. The northern pike is a very aggressive predator. They don't like to live in groups with other fish, they are very territorial and like to live alone. Their behavior is closely affected by weather conditions. The biggest Northern Pike caught in Rhode Island weighed 35 pounds and measured 47.5 inches.

Fun Facts About Rhode Island Fish

1 - The official state fish of Rhode Island is the Striped Bass, adopted in 2000 due to its popularity as a sport fish in the region.

2 - Unlike other fish, the brook trout lack teeth on the roof of their mouth. They rely on their bottom teeth to grab food.

3 - The lake sturgeon is the granddaddy of all fish. They can live up to 100 years and weigh up to 300 pounds in some areas.

4 - The largest, officially recognized freshwater fish caught in Rhode Island is a 35-pound, 47.5-inch Northern Pike.

5 - Key game fish include largemouth/smallmouth bass, striped bass, northern pike, and various trout (brook, brown, rainbow).

6 - The American Eel has an odd habit of wrapping its slimy tail around the hand or arm of anglers who catch one. Not to worry, it won't hurt you.

7 – Rhode Island is home to more than 70 species of fish found in its fresh and brackish waters. This includes minnows and other smaller fish.

Author Page

Billy Grinslott & Kinsey Marie Books

Copyright, All Rights Reserved

ISBN – 9781968228682

Thanks